yellowrocket

yellowrocket

POEMS

TODD BOSS

W • W • NORTON & COMPANY • New York • London

For information about permission to reproduce
selections from this book, write to Permissions,
W. W. Norton & Company, Inc.,
500 Fifth Avenue, New York, NY 10110

For information about special discounts for bulk purchases,
please contact W. W. Norton Special Sales at
specialsales@wwnorton.com or 800-233-4830

Manufacturing by Courier Westford
Book design by Antonina Krass
Production manager: Andrew Marasia

Library of Congress Cataloging-in-Publication Data

Boss, Todd.
Yellowrocket : poems / Todd Boss. — 1st ed.
p. cm.
ISBN 978-0-393-06768-2
I. Title.
PS3602.O8375Y45 2008
811'.6—dc22

                                                    2008023239

W. W. Norton & Company, Inc.
500 Fifth Avenue, New York, N.Y. 10110
www.wwnorton.com

W. W. Norton & Company Ltd.
Castle House, 75/76 Wells Street, London W1T 3QT

1 2 3 4 5 6 7 8 9 0

FOR BETH

Contents

O N E

Ruin   13

Yellowrocket   15

Blessed with Trump and Wild   19

How It Must Have Been for Him   21

Another Hand   22

Wood Burning   23

The Plat Book   25

Jimmy Stewart Reading *Winnie-the-Pooh*
    on RCA Camden Hi-Fidelity   28

Why I'll Never Be an Artist   31

T W O

Inventory   35

Advance   36

Not Crash, Nor Roar   38

Turbulence: Three Exercises   39

In the Morning We Found   42

As in a Sudden Downpour, When,   43

The Trees—They Were Once Good Men   44

The Issue   46

The World Does Not Belong to You,

    Though You Belong to the World,   48

THREE

The Hush of the Very Good   51

More So   52

Don't Come Home   53

Tangled Hangers and All,   54

Wish   55

The Deeper the Dictionary   56

Mess   57

Six Nights in a Hotel   59

They Thought They Knew Me Here   61

FOUR

The Wallpaper   65

My House Is Small and Almost   66

To Be Alone Again in the Thick Skin   67

Patiently, the Partial Brides   69

She Rings Me Up   71

Worst Work   76

The Truth   77

What Yesterday Appeared a Scar   78
A Man Stares into the Same Painting
    Day after Day   79

F I V E

Things, Like Dogs   83
My Son Climbs In   85
Ere We Are Aware   86
Nocturne   88
Chimney   90
White Ash Goes Up at a Touch   92
Icicles   93
To Wind a Mechanical Toy   94
Constellations   100

S I X

The Day Un-Dims   103
My Son Puts His Pants On Backwards,   104
My Joy Doubled   106
The Day Is Gray and the Lake   108
How Smokes the Smolder   110
A Deer   112
To a Wild Rose   113
One Can Miss Mountains   114
Enough   116

Acknowledgments   117

Notes   119

Thanks   121

ONE

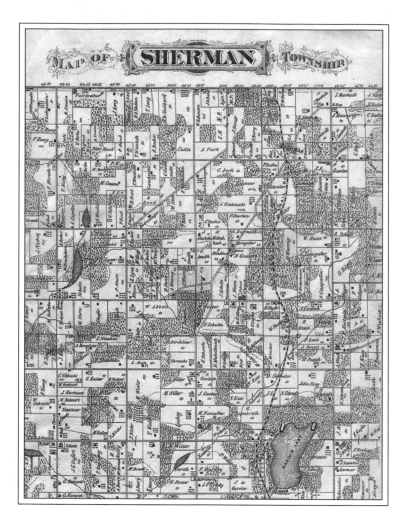

Ruin

was rumored

to be rooming
                        up the road
                              where

a neighbor's barn'd
burned down.

            Their heyday
                              a payday
away,

Pride,
    Ruin's bride-to-be,

                    paced our property
                        in the long

laced gowns
    of afternoons,

                        while Ruin
                        rode shotgun
                    in Dad's old Ford

and pulled the wheel
    hard toward
                        cabarets.

13

Dad had
work, but

       Ruin had ways.

Yellowrocket

Filthy, but still of good
tilth, our new bargain 80
(40 high, 40 hinter)
made us instantly
wealthy with rubbish.

Never buy a farm
in winter. For years,
my mother stood
by my father's side
in thickets choked

with tractor parts
and bedcoil and
cried. Whether grief
or shame or the fact
that people could be

such pigs more
upset her, I never
knew. Didn't matter.
Whatever it was
filled up our

quarter-ton Ford a
hundred times over.
The work was clay
deep, the debt was
north slope steep.

We could've driven
State Highway 27
to the local dump in
our sleep. I grew up in
boiled wool jackets,

thinking soil smelled
like brushfire smoke.
Had holes been coins,
our gloves and boots
would've jangled.

Unwitting heirs, we'd
come into a garden
overgrown with plastic
diapers and broken
furniture tangled in

burdock and brambles
and thistle. We'd split
with family and moved
a hundred miles, and
the gamble's payout

was piles of bent nails
and moldering shingle.
Some messes called
for rake, others shovel.
Either way, by dusk of

day we were down
on our knees picking
window glass shards
from the muck. If we
rested, we rested from

wresting long twists
of rusted barbed wire
from deepening kinks
of birches. Primal
was our desire to take

that junk pile back
from the skunk and
the snake and the rat.
We were the unsung
angels of our portion

of the plat. And for
all that, on Sundays
the Lord gave us halos
of hat hair and gnats,
and then, in due season:

the apple's blossom,
forest floors dappled
with trillium, fields
of tall corn, a barn not
yet fallen, views of the

countryside patterned
with drifting pollen,
berries by the bucketful,
the otherworldly lull
of the breeze in our

break of white pines,
5-wire fences posted
in good straight lines,
the easy spirals
of the golden eagles

that nested in our
hardwoods' crowns,
the kind of sky
in which a small boy
drowns, our health,

and a feel for the earth
indistinct from
scorn. Call it love,
but if you call it love,
call it a love that

persisted, that
stained the palms
and reeked when
you pulled it,
like yellowrocket.

Blessed with Trump and Wild

or crap, but no less blessed,
my grandpas, when at last retired,
thumped the table card over card
at nickel-a-trick pinochle and
partners canasta, the same decks
pounded, bent, and shuffled soft

as their flannel shirts. As a boy,
they often held me on their laps,
their arms about me, so I could see
their hoards. Their buckles poked
and I fiddled with their braces.
I studied their hewn and stubbled
faces and watched them push
thick figures onto envelope backs
from a pencil nub, then rub them out
for a proper score. I had no words

for how it felt to sit so intimate with
kings, their hearts, their diamonds
fairly dripping through their knuckles
when they dealt. They'd handled
teams of horses in their time and
tilled a thousand acres roll on roll,
and raised whole families out of black
Wisconsin dirt, and on that map
I was a speck. A silt fault in the river.

I had no words for how I felt, nor
will I ever, for in that flicker naught
was said that couldn't be said with
a click of a tongue or a snap of a
card or a snicker. Naught could be
bargained, either. Too soon, one
went out. And then, to the man, their
good hands folded and folded forever.

How It Must Have Been
for Him

Their life was a bicker.

In fifty hard years on the farm together
pleasure never pulled the plow,

so how, at the break of the day she died
did it feel to find her unawake
at last the worse for wear
   tucked beside him in a bunch
   her slippers on the floor
   the thermostat down
   eggs unbroken in their icebox divots
   the Marshfield paper at the step
   and chores to be done

how rode his farmer's fingers
in the dial-holes of the slow, foundering 9
and the two brief 1's

and in which of fifty fields
did he find the words
to say to the end of the line
not her name, not
a pronoun merely
but *my wife* . . .

my wife has died, send someone . . .

Another Hand

Here—here's a day—
and here—here's another,

says God feeling chancy,
says God feeling grand.

Hell—here—look—
a stack of days—a week,

says God nonchalant,
a penny candy in his cheek,

the glimmer in his eye
never giving him away.

Good old God,
he's a player alright.

Across a blue cloth
as he antes them over

the gold coins shimmer
from his fat black purse.

Wood Burning

To my father, a
woods is not a
woods without a
wood pile in it, a
brush mess near it
where the lesser
limbs landed. To
my father, *season*
is a verb, a reason
not to disturb one
cord or another.
I swear his veins
run bar chain oil.
To my father, no
carpet is as royal
as a sawdust trail
in the muddy soil.
All that smacks of
riches is as air to
him, compared to
the ring of his axe
in the hills and the
ditches around his
shacks, and those
stacks banked up
against a future
winter's weather.
And before we're
awake, he's back
at that brick altar,

opening the cold
and stubborn iron
heart of the house,
turning the fact of
newsprint and tinder
into a kind of prayer
for our warming—
his first tender act
of the morning.

The Plat Book

cast our farm
and neighbors'
farms as flat,

our last names
spattered across
their scant

shapes in slant
caps, our land-
scape cropped

and spiral bound.
I found I could
leaf through

miles of ground
in a snap, from
town to town-

ship and hilltop
to millpond,
every dotted

logging lane
and back alley
kink in plain

black ink hand-
plotted. To think
what thought'd

gone into that
odd elevation!
To me it was a

revelation that
the land could
be recorded and

recorded free
of all topography,
distorted by

the tax man's
idiosyncratic
iconography.

For this was
his, not our Eau
Claire County.

Ours had airy
view and hue
and landmarks,

oaks and willows
and windmills
and cattle in it.

No, we couldn't
have survived
a minute

on that non-soil,
an *O* where our
undrawn

house and barn
and all our toil
would go.

Jimmy Stewart Reading
Winnie-the-Pooh
on RCA Camden Hi-Fidelity

was my introduction
to poetry. Also Sterling
Holloway doing
Peter and the Wolf and
Mother Goose rhymes

with the Camarata Players
at thirty-three-and-a-third
RPM. Can I remember
word-for-word Paul

Wing's rendition of *The
Little Engine that Could*?
I think I can. I ran
those records till the hiss
was a surf. I knew by rote

when to lift our stereo's
cherrywood lid
and bend inside and guide
the needle over skips.
I learned to ride hayrake
around our eighty acres faking

hay fever so I could
stack them five high
in my room and listen
for an hour. Why? Their
voices. I craved their
voices, savored the way their
voices wrapped around

each syllable delicious.
It was Speech 101,
Academy of Dramatic Arts,
Fall Creek, Wisconsin,
nothing like it for a hundred miles
in any direction. Less a class

than private tutelage:
Stewart, Holloway, Wing
& Associates at my service

daily after school. I studied
every nuance, every inflection.
They had rhythm.

When they read their parts,
my lips moved with them.
What luck I was their pupil.
Proverbial needle! I'd

learned to whistle by listening
to the jay, and I knew
by the day I turned ten
that I too would be
a narrator someday, like them.

Why I'll Never Be an Artist

My mother says I'll never be an artist because I haven't suffered enough. She has just finished telling her rock-picker's story.

My cousin is an artist too, and he's sitting on the couch, in my living room. His mother is my mother's sister. She agrees. *That's right*, she says. *You two know nothing of suffering.*

Nobody says anything then. Except History, which grudgingly opens its case and starts drawing the old bow back and forth across the strings.

For forty-five years, the Buddha repeated: "I teach only suffering and the transformation of suffering."

Our mothers wipe their noses. They have been crying. They are still mourning their own mother's dying. How little they knew her. The things they never told her! There is so much they didn't understand.

And into their eyes comes a light too lonely not to recognize.

TWO

Inventory

We had Kris Kristofferson's
Me and Bobby McGee

in vinyl.
We had vegetable

barley soup in
Mason jars and plenty

of candles and cakes
of lye soap.

We had firewood
by the cord.

My father had some
muscle and an

Allis Chalmers tractor.
Autumn's apples

were in the larder,
the guns were locked,

the freezer was stocked,
the garden was weeded,

we thought we had all
that we needed.

Advance

With a squeal, the already
otherworldly broadcast
stuttered,
                    scattered,
                                    leaving
only a tattered hiss.

                                    At first
my father's fingers
                    fussed
the dial of our radio,
                                    signals
fritzed as a flintless lighter,

then he leaned in closer,
intent on
                    teasing
                                    the news
we needed
                    out of that box.

I never saw him touch more
slightly anything or anyone,
all his
        fingertips navigating
in and out of
                    nonsense for
the lifeline of our lives,
before
        swiping it off.

                    Now
no more news was ours but
the storm's dark musings
on the matter.

                    Even last
fall's fruit, jarred in the root
cellar just around the corner,
sucked
        its cupped lids
                        tighter.

Not Crash, Nor Roar

but chug of train is how survivors
tend to explain the score of an oncoming twister. Queer,

to compare a work of nature to so
tame a thing as steel wheels riding parallel rails,

but isn't that how terror assails us: by masquerading
its powers as everyday things, spinning clouds

into funnels, towers into tunnels?
And do we ascertain the sound as locomotive

while the tornado's rough tongue touches down,
or do we apply the metaphoric construction

only *after* the destruction blows town?
And if the latter, doesn't the sound describe

not terror's arrival, but safety's departure,
as it rumbles over the switches of our survival?

Does it ever get easier for us, the lovelorn,
hugging ourselves against the strain

of being left behind,
on a platform,

in the rain?

Turbulence: Three Exercises

1. A SQUALL

will rail
at a westerly
wall awhile,
will reel, will

roll like a
wheel, mile
over mile up
hill, down

dale, will
loose all hell
and finally
drown just

east of town,
like an old hired
hand grown
tired of it all.

2. A FIGHT

might nightly
light like
lightning
any frightening

sight in white
reverse, might
write it on our lids
like a curse,

might blind,
or worse,
might bind us
to each other

like horses
hitched abreast,
or like the bright
black boxes

tethered
tight against
the pitches
of hearses.

3. A QUAKE

may break
the foundation
of a lake or an
ocean

wide open,
and lighten,
according
to the space

station *Grace*,
even gravity's
place in
the universe,

plates shifting
mid drift in
order to absorb
it, but, from

orbit, appear
as peaceful
as a face
at a wake.

In the Morning We Found

forty acres of oaks

torn to the ground.

The storm

had spattered barn,

house, shed, whole

farm in red mud

and a leafy shred.

My parents walked,

alone and paired,

through the weird

carnage, mourning

—downed trees still

green and breathing

as soon they would

no more—fallen

as in a war.

As in a Sudden Downpour, When,

out on the town together, men
won't wait until the harder
shower's over, nor cower, nor dodge
for cover, awning to awning, as one
would certainly do on one's own,
but troop on as before, or slower,
as if the weather were warfare,
every street a trench, their amble
in the drench a marching order—

don't we too, arm in arm on a
foreign city's cobbles, stumble
from welfare into harm on cue,
our duty to perform, but in no
hurry, drunk on courage, gauging
only a faraway worry in the rage?
Don't we too slosh from age
to age and curtain to curtain,
awash in camaraderie, our
eager number our only cover?

The Trees—They Were Once Good Men

and good women,
who for whatever
reason were never
given the keys to
heaven,

and who stand now

arms outstretched
to one another, some
entangled, some even

grown together, in
more than solidarity
but still afraid to fall
in love again.
       From
these, in this thin
stand here one sees
one's vulnerability:
one's slender life,
one's limbs lifted
high.
    The air.
       Sun-
riddled good-byes.
The wood.
     Listen—

Can you hear your
deepest prayer?

Your furthest flung
flitter of shame?
Your heaviest sigh,
sung like a name?

No.
    No, nor can I.

The Issue

of tears my mother
cleared with tissue

was never resolved.
 In her rescue,
years

after the first fell,
 aren't we all
still involved,

my sisters
 and I? It burned
our ears,

salt in a cut,
 to hear her,
hear her

cry like that, her
 voice now
fierce, now

clotted with contempt,
 now yielding,
meek

as a barn kitten's
 mews.
At our old oak table

crumpled, she
 folded, unfolded
the weak

white flags as if
 (even as it
dissolved)

she were reading,
 rereading
the news.

The World Does Not Belong to You,
Though You Belong to the World,

for this is not a marriage,
living. Only you have
given your hand and
climbed into the carriage
of Morning. Where do you
think you're going? Morning
owes you nothing. She is

fickle, she is strong. Only
to Morning does Morning
belong. As she takes you
into the day, onto the old
wide way of the world, she
sings so intimate a song you
may begin to believe she

loves you. You may even
come to believe you somehow
guide her along sometimes,
but you are wrong.
You think you are a pitcher
taking the mound, but it's
the other way around.

THREE

The Hush of the Very Good

You can tell by how he lists
                                    to let her
kiss him, that the getting, as he gets it,
is good.
                    It's good in the sweetly salty,
deeply thirsty way that a sea-fogged
rain is good after a summer-long bout
of inland drought.
                              And you know it
when you see it, don't you? How it
drenches what's dry, how the having
of it quenches.
                          There is a grassy inlet
where your ocean meets your land, a slip
that needs a certain kind of vessel,
                                                and
when that shapely skiff skims in at last,
trimmed bright, mast lightly flagging
left and right,
                        then the long, lush reeds
of your longing part, and soft against
the hull of that bent wood almost im-
perceptibly brushes a luscious hush
the heart heeds helplessly—
                                          the hush
of the very good.

More So

Whoever they are, these friends of ours
seem not the least self-conscious
sharing the indiscreet details
of how they met and how they courted

half as long ago as we. They purr
like cats lapping cream from the same
little bowl, their whiskers nixing.
(Is it really so simple for some—

their stories no more complex
than TV listings?)
                    It comes our turn.

I try: "For us, love was always complex,"
and everything changes, like a badly

timed commercial. My wife agrees,
thank heaven, though she won't get a hearing.

"Love is complex," someone repeats,
clearing plates and offering: "More to drink?"

but it's late, and more so than they think.

Don't Come Home

ranks first among
the worst things
someone you love
can say. Not even
the common *I
hate you* does
the damage *Don't
come home* will
do. You can live
with *I hate you,*
same as you live
with the past.
You abide it. *I
hate you* in fact
can be worth
coming home to,
like anything built
to last. *I hate you*
may be the mythical
two in the bush
the bird in the hand
is worth, while
Don't come home,
by contrast, *is*
that first bird,
caught bird, scared
to sing its song,
percussive wings
held fist-fast just
so long.

Tangled Hangers and All,

my wardrobe swirls through the hall and
down the stairwell
like sails in a squall, a surge of limbs,

all flailing, sweaters
unfurling as if in the falling waters of our
marriage rolling,

our better days like lighter weather apparently
over forever,
my wife stark raving as if to save

her life, while I
stand idly by as the river swells deep and high
with necktie twists,

balled fists of socks, a bandy-legged affair
of thermal underwear,
suit jackets shoulder to shoulder in trysts.

For a quarter of an hour
it goes on like this, her rage a naked force
of ice cold air

dropping hard off a shelf of high pressure,
and grasping there
the hand of disaster as a natural course,

everything around us
—the kids, the coming morning, the house—
pounding in its pulse.

Wish

You've never not been negative.
I wouldn't know you if
you weren't. You never wish
but in the subjunctive,
candles to the frosting burnt.

The Deeper the Dictionary

the more complex the lexicon.

Take you and me.
The sheets like pages, pulled on

and torn off in a rage!
The long-dead languages! Ah—

but the core of our love
is six thousand sheets down!

And here we are, shamming
counterpanes, when

the mattress, the box spring,
coil with origins.

Mess

I was banging our empty dinner dishes
self-righteously down on the kitchen
counter when she let the water run over.

"You asked me how," she said.
                              I said,
"How *what?*" and reached to shut
the tap, but she stopped me, her nails
in my veins. The water was rolling
down the cabinetry in steaming glass
panes. We were already standing in a
puddle. I struggled, but she stayed me.
Her blue eyes on me, we stared
hard through the clogged pipe
of our marriage while the sink water
wept across the linoleum. It was raining
in the basement by now. I reached with
my other hand, but she caught that too,
and then we were joined like dancers
in some modern performance thing.

I wrenched away from her, squaring
off. I was pissed. "How *what?*" I hissed.

"Like this!" she said, and her open
hand slapping flat on the counter made
a spritz of the spill there: *splat!* "You
asked me how you should love me."
Her hand on stone went *slap! slap! slap!*
At last she tore her eyes away.

                        I went
for the tap. I grabbed some towels. I
started to sop up the mess.

                        "Like this,"
she said again, as if I didn't understand.
And that was when she turned on the
tears. It was as if there was no bottom
at the source of her distress. And yes,
I'll dry them all if it takes me years.

Six Nights in a Hotel

1

My wife and I

a mile apart

2

A splurge last
night, and so,
from Styrofoam:
cold inch of steak,
toughened rind
of baked potato,
puck of bread
for my breakfast

3

Crusty screws
affix the soap dish

Spack of caulk
slops a crack of tile

In the mirror
a slipshod smile
unglues

4

In the pool
I ply a solitude
3 ft. deep

end
to end

5

My pride
is a fire
retardant blanket

It covers but it
does not warm

6

Out in the lot
cars wait as if

post-hitched,

noses where
there ought
to be grass

They Thought They Knew Me Here

till they realized I look exactly
like another one of their regulars
who prefers the same corner, and
then it was confusing: Did they know

me or not? Did they know him?
Or were we now some amalgam
of two regulars, one's food allergies
ascribed to the other, one a heavy

drinker, the other a lousy tipper?
I sit down and the bartender says,
Lemme guess . . . and guesses
what the other me likes for lunch.

I'm not the man with whom my wife
fell in love, and now I'll never be
again. The water under the bridge
runs milkshake thick, and when I lean

out over the edge, another guy looks
vaguely back, reversed in a quick of silt,
like someone trying to catch my eye
to place an order, to pay a bill.

The waitresses avoid me. I'm guilty
for another man's reasons, complicit
in a conspiracy of circumstance.
So now I'm afraid to go to that café,

afraid I'll run right into my parallel.
Is he afraid of me? We've ruined it for
each other, apparently, living this double
life. Did we think we'd pull it off?

Longfellow Café, Minneapolis, 2006

FOUR

The Wallpaper

says hello.
            The wallpaper
misses you something
awful.
            The wallpaper
can't stop wondering when
you were thinking of
coming home.
                        The clock's
moved on.
                        The sink's ten
million tears are dry.
Our floors have gotten
over you, or so they
                        claim
and claim.
            The windows
clearly feel the same.
But call me.
                        Call me
soon, my love,
and tell me
                        what to say
next time
                        the fading and
tedious
                        wallpaper whispers
your
            beautiful household
name.

My House Is Small and Almost

a hundred years old. Inside,
the oaken posts and beams
make the living room seem
like a glade. When friends
pronounce it comfortable,
it's 1910 that comforts them,
and nothing I have done.

There must be a room
in the human heart
that's older than the body.
And it's good to be there
in that foursquare cathedral
where nothing has changed
since before we were made.

To Be Alone Again in the Thick Skin

of this low-slung bungalow house,
August overcast and waning,
windows open to the breathings
of the distant interstate passing,
you and the kids on some errand,
no note on the kitchen counter,
the workday done, my computer
on and waiting, I feel so helpless
against a tide of emotion I can
only identify as a melancholy joy.
When I was a boy come home
from school to the farm alone,
my father working, my mom with
my sister to a lesson or something,
I would pass through all the rooms
in a daze, lingering, gazing in all
the mirrors, lying down on all
the beds, trying myself on for size
in every doorway, every hall. Or
I would wander the farm itself,
the lawns, the lanes, the fields.
There was no highway there to
trouble the sound of being alone.
The only noise was wind if there
was wind, or plane if overhead
a plane. I didn't know it then,
but we lived beneath the pattern
of flights from MSP International
to points northeast and pan-Atlantic,
and though they were so far up in

the air, their thin roar glimmered
in your ears if you strained hard
to hear. It never occurred to me
that one day I'd be tired of flying.
That the thrill of passing again over
my own hometown would finally   ,
be lost on me. Looking back on
that clueless boy, I pity him
for who he became. For isn't there
something lonely about a life
that wasn't in the least foreseen?
I live in someone else's city, in
someone else's house, it seems.
It's as if one day I stumbled into a
giant jumble sale of dreams, and
left with my arms loaded, caring
only that I got some good bargains.
I'm not saying I don't love my life.
Your heart and this city and this house
are the only places I can imagine
belonging. But isn't that just it?
In, through the screens of our lives,
the song of the world outside comes
thronging in all its unexpected
discord. And we call that chaos
home, despite everything we love.

Patiently, the Partial Brides

in the bridal shop window

wait.

The shop's
closed up for the night

and yet

they wait
with the diligence

of the dead

and the mis-
understood.—See how she's

lost her head,

how she her arms, how she
is nothing but a shelf

display,

as if there'd been a tussle
for a thrown bouquet.

This one

is nothing but a bride-
shaped

cage.

They stand around on needles
and pins,

strangled

by the silences they sing.
The morning will cue no

voluntary.

There is no telling
for whom the little front

door bell will ring.

She Rings Me Up

four frozen dinners
and a pint of politically
correct ice cream.

I say real casual,
"I don't need a
bag, or nothing."

She looks at me
like I'm a fruit
with no sticker,

then mutters,
"Anything."

"Huh?" I say.

And she says, "*I*
don't need a bag, or
anything."

I'm completely
confused. It doesn't
make sense. Why
would my cashier
need or not need
a bag, when *I'm*
the one carrying
the groceries in
this relationship?

I just stand there
while she swipes
my Visa card and
cups her tattooed
hand over the slot
in the register
where the receipt
comes out.

I say, "I don't
quite follow you."

"You said *nothing . . .*"
she says, and winks,
though her wink
doesn't match her
tone, and now I'm

doubly confused (I
hadn't said nothing
since before I'd
said anything to this
woman, with her
multiple piercings
and her strange way
of talking) ". . . not

nothing," she's
saying now. "It's
anything," but I'm
no longer listening.

I'm tired. It's been
a long week, it's
getting on evening,
and I skipped lunch
this afternoon. And
I'm in the middle
of a difficult time.

At that very moment,
inspiration kicks in,

and I realize it's a
guy/girl thing.

Of course. That's it.

She's talking about
love. It's no wonder
I don't understand her.

She hands me
a pen taped with a
pink plastic daisy.

"It's your diction,"
she says softly.

I check my fly before
signing my name.

She's right, it's my
diction. I'm back in
the game. I remember
this as flirting: two
people in a confusion
transaction. It's been
a long time since
I spoke this tongue.

I decide to take a paper
bag after all, just
to throw her, just to
keep the dervish
of the conversation
whirling while I
think of something
cool and cryptic and
casual to say.

I shake it out with a
bang, and collect my
frozen things, their
boxes all frosty.

Have I been right
to believe myself
attractive, despite
so much rejection?
Will I still get a
chance to claim,
if only innocently,
what might be mine?

Then she says, "Hi,"

and I say "Hi"—before
I see she's talking
to the next guy in line.

Worst Work

God wrote a poem about me,
which should have been flattering,
but He let me read it,
and it was awful.

And what was I going to say?
Far be it from me to hurt God's feelings.
"Hey," I said, "that's pretty good."
Well, it wasn't completely untrue.

What a bad word, *good,*
where creation is concerned.

I guess I might have given
the great provocateur a fight,
but I know too much
about the art of making art.
I owe it to my faith to give the old fart
the benefit of doubt.
It's hard to write a poem
about someone you love,
for one thing. And for another,
it's hard to take a lesson from
your own worst work.

The Truth

is a chewy
treat, like
toffee, only
less sweet,
and slightly
nutty, like
birch bark,
with a salty
aftertaste as
steely as a
flint-spark,
best doused
with straight
whiskey or
dark coffee.

What Yesterday Appeared a Scar

of brilliant green
in the icy lake, today
arcs blue across its face and far.
And where this morning
still is frozen,
coming hours will warm until
the water's softer
nature's finally chosen.

Half my life is gone
to others' business,
which, well done or not, it
matters not but that it's gone
and won't be gotten back.

And half my love is wasted too.
Wasted not on you, where all my
deeps and deeps of love
are dammed and so belong,
but on loving you
wrong. My sorrow
is tomorrow's only season,
and it comes on now

like this cold thaw comes
upon the lake,
or like a soft song one sings to sing
the past to sleep,
only to keep it wide awake.

A Man Stares into the
Same Painting Day after Day

for years—a row of two-story houses.
And then one day something appears
in a window that wasn't there before.

A curled cat or an ornate crack or a
stack of folded linens, it's hard to tell.

And a window is opened in him, and
he is placed upon his understanding's
gritty granite sill. His life has a fresh
smell. It tingles.
               Nearby, a neglected
load of regrets on his clothesline is dry
and he tries one on, and it feels okay.

He goes into the world by a new way,
reborn. And all because of what he saw
in that fictional window over his mantel,
that cross-hatch, that patch of morning
sun, that—in another hour—was gone.

FIVE

Things, Like Dogs

I came home last night to find that my
laptop had crawled up onto the table

in anticipation of my being there,
and the piano light had switched itself on,

and two eggs had cracked themselves
into a skillet on the stove. It was odd

because I never make eggs for dinner,
but beyond that, it was kind of nice.

Kind of nice to know that things,
like dogs, grow fond and want

to be had, to be used, to be played.
I stood in the emptying window light,

my shirtfront swelling with gratitude.
I was just about to say something aloud

to the contents of my house, something
grand and at the same time tender, when

the first word caught
in my throat. I stood there alone

till at last a chair I hadn't known about
nudged the backs of my knees

and a dusty Kleenex sneezed itself out
of a nearby box I hadn't put there. Had

I slept I might have dreamed of rocking
gently under the stars on a ship whose

crew was foreign, whose maps
were thumbed in sand on deck each morning.

My mantel clock rang out a warning,
and later I found this poem at the back door,

looking softly up at me and wagging
its little tail.

My Son Climbs In

beside me, falls asleep
in a lump, all his jump

and shimmy plumb
run out. He's about

as wide and as deep
as a pillow, plumped.

And I—propped
slumped and reading,

needing no one to
tuck me in, needing

nothing really—
eventually I take

to nodding, nodding
with all I know and have

known, toward the un-
known. Later I wake,

my book in my lap,
the lamp still bright,

to find him grinding
his tiny white teeth

with all his might.

Ere We Are Aware

we err. We err
        in open air, dare-

devil as a swallow's
        swerve. We err

with verve. Our errors serve
        as bearings

as we flare and dive
        and flounder.

We scare away our lovers
        and declare

a territory where before
        there wasn't any.

Later we share our feelings.
        Say we're

sorry. Swear to be
        more careful.

Oh, we show our showy words
        like colors

and then, in a flurry of ever
        rarer, ever

braver aerials, there
           we are again,

famished birds wheeling
           over burials.

Nocturne

We tend
to sleep better

when the clock
is wound

than we do
when it's all

wound down.
I don't know

why we settle
to the sound.

Somehow
the regular

click and chime
of passing time,

like water, turns
a waterwheel

that turns a gear
that turns a stone

that turns upon
another stone

and fine and
 finer in between

our dreams like grain
 are ground.

Chimney

We have lived our lives around this chimney.
Given it our kindle, our blaze,
our bounty.

Up this chimney chased our days.
Scarcity and plenty
have risen there.

Up this chimney, as in a single breath,
were drawn the crisp winter air, and the wet
spring air, and the air of summer,
sweet and salty.

We have not held dear enough
the warm slant of morning or the soft
evening light. They have drifted
into a nether air, and gone.

Gone have gone the sounds
of those at table, their laughter. Dinner prayer.
The argument, the song. The candle's flicker.
Gone.

Ice in a pitcher, smell of ginger. Bread from
the oven, mulled cider.

Gone to their ends went our dreams of more.
We have poured them up this chimney
with a roar!

Come! Sit with me here, by the fire, friends,
and remember—

                    after Edip Cansever

White Ash Goes Up at a Touch

while the black oak

takes coaxing.
That popping and

whistling? Yellow
birch and red pine.

Difference
might for now define,

but soon the whole
church is chanting

at the same time,
flame splashing

bright from the dirty
bucket of the earthly,

roaring likeness
and only likeness

into the bottomless
cool of the night . . .

Icicles

are made of melt.
The same course
that makes them
takes them away.

They stay as long
as the temperature
lets them, and go
by the same way,

and in the same
direction. Their
art consists of
nothing but their

own creation and
destruction. On
that intersection
their existence

hangs—as hangs
a heart by how
and for how long
what's felt is felt.

To Wind a Mechanical Toy

i   is to mind it. To wind between
    finger and thumb a thing too

    inconsequential to mention
    is to find the essential tension

    that divides the living from
    the dumb. To grind some gizmo

    into usefulness, the ratchet
    catching against the paul

    (much the way a match scratched
    against a wall of flint is minted

    into flame), is to come directly
    into a kind of small (but

    no less existential) bind:
    To bring a thing into motion

    (whether it be a diversion or an
    ocean) is to draw one's bow

    across resistant strings
    (and yes, I speak for the Creator

    when I broach this notion),
    for everything's radical that is.

To exist at all is to feel the clock-
steady undertow of inertia.

My mother had a music box
I loved when I was a boy.

I loved to twist its comical key
and set its tiny tines into play

across its rubbled metal drum.
I loved the way, ere long,

its song lost the muscle of its
wound copper coil and how

sublimely sound surrendered
to a well-oiled but untimely

end. The pressures of applied
and implied stress impressed me.

The tune was "Edelweiss," I
think. (*Bless   my*

home
                    land
for-
                              . . .)

Repeatedly melody's tendency
to resolve succumbed

to a far more commonplace
dependency: the exquisite

frictions of applied physics.

ii Yesterday a friend asked me,

    Why is it so hard to be happy?
    She asked it very generously,

    but I didn't have the energy
    to crank my pretty little theory

    out of its filigree box. *Life
    sucks*, I said. We laughed, but

    even our laughter, clunky from the
    dusty hurdy-gurdies of our hearts,

    was half over before it started,
    and in truth it wasn't a genuine

    mirth. (You know the worth of a
    good laugh when you have one.

Often I find I get one in the car,
about five hours into a trip. Any

quip or observation or country
song can set me off by then.

The best laughs are deep down
in the odometer.) I don't know

what to say to her. Shouldn't
things get easier? Why don't we

love better fragrant than fresh?
That romance traditionally

blooms in *spring* is one of love's
greatest plays on words—a twist

that untwists as trysts turn to
marriages, marriages to mists.

iii   For Christmas last year my boy
      got a Schilling tin toy from

      Santa Claus. Guess who got
      more play time out of its

windup spiral elevator, chute,
and tumblers? These gadgets

aren't actually made for children,
so of course by New Year's Eve

I had it broken, but that's when
the real pleasure began:

to find a glue that favors tin
was my first endeavor. Then,

to reinstall the fallen platform
not just where, but better than

it had been mounted before,
that was the second. Then,

when the glue was still drying:
trial runs one and two and three;

the adjustments they required;
the removal of the part and its

re-reinstallation; trial runs four,
five, six, and seven . . . I finally

had it up and running, but who
cares? By then I'd had my fun,

all alone at the dining room
table, the kids asleep upstairs,

Times Square crowds counting
down, and another ball falling

from the past and into the future
through the gimcrack contraption

we call our monthly calendar,
but which is actually the rise

and fall, the ease and pull,
of the solar, lunar, and stellar

mechanicals of the universe,
locked in their epic argument over

which is bigger, which is stronger,
who started it,

and how, if ever,
it will end.

Constellations

You rare!—
          You shooting star!—

You comet!—
          How can I connect

my love to you, elusive

dot-to-dot,
          reclusive rocket?—

All I do is chase you, even when

we're face to face.
          Loving you,

I'm trying to trace—
          in daylight—

constellations!—

SIX

The Day Un-Dims

before it lightens,
like something

emerging. A fish
swims upwards

out of darkness
before it begins

to glimmer; so
day is drawn

from depth, as if
a morning were

just an idea
that nobody's

quite yet hit upon.
And then, and

only then, does it
dawn.

My Son Puts His Pants On Backwards,

fly
in the rear,
and I
tie my tie

quickly,
cockeye,
and out we
trip into

the great
disheveled
throng fan-
tastic, tails

untucked,
his mitten
in my glove.
Don't love

dress funny
sometimes?
And shouldn't
it be sin

to wear so
carelessly
such finery?
It fills me

up with
sympathy!
I swear
we'd lose our

hearts if
they weren't
with elastic
and butterfly

pin
clasped safely
in.

My Joy Doubled

to drive my daughter
through the jeweled
morning light
this morning:

joy to sigh,
"What a lovely morning!"
and see the glimmer
in her eye
in the rear-view mirror
as our light went green,

and joy to show her how
the ochre sunrise hadn't
yet washed down
from the cross
on the steeple
at the top of town.

The temperature
was three degrees,
the bank sign said.
"Wake up, old Mr. Sun,"
we called as if he were
our corner grocer,
not the ember burling
distant crowns.

A mile we rode in silence
while the nickel-purple
crystal of the world
was poured with light.

I need to think she saw it all
as it sped by—
the rink in spun
chain link, the outlet mall
in mist—and loved
the pinks and golds
as I do. She is so young.
If I can't train her eyes
to love, how else then
praise the lapidary,
who cuts our days
like diamonds
from the carbon cold above?

The Day Is Gray and the Lake

shifts, mercurial,
like modeling clay,

the million thumbs
of wind at work upon it,

the artist unable to come
to a single conclusion.

Just what shape *should*
this cold lake take

this morning?
And the trees surrounding?

The maker can't
make up his mind, always

fussing. He shuffles
the shoreline shadows

like a paint-chip deck.
The reeds.

The nervous birds.
The toads, forever lost

on mud's malleable maps.
Everything's a mess

and genius all at once,
a school for unruliness.

Even the stones second-
guess themselves, eroding.

And there: a wash of sunshine,
and some people, boating.

How Smokes the Smolder

at neck, at
shoulder, that

stokes a man
as he grows

older. Nothing
rages, nothing

fumes. No one
races through

the rooms,
alarmed. How

casually he's
armed. How

gradually arises
what surprises

in his mirrors.
Unawares, as

fall runs colder,
pulls he only

slightly tighter
his good wool

sweater, thinner
than ever now

at elbow,
at shoulder.

A Deer

It seems to me to be again as if
our twenty years were no more than a dream—

This morning, driving in the steam of dawn
in an autumn woods, I happened upon
a yearling deer that was, unlike her tawny
sisters, a brilliant white. All white and white
and white she was, a great astonishment
of white—
                            her body a flag, a flame of snow
in the bower, she was a glow, a ghost
in the mist around her. And oh, my dear, how
I wished you were there! She wore herself
so regally I thought of you immediately.

She trembled so to see me slow to the gravel
and halt. I had to wait her out, so filled
with praise was I, my heart. What grace,
what art, what eloquence she bore! Though
no less and no more a deer than any deer
in the forest, still it seemed these trees were
holier for her being there, in the recitative
of a leafing breeze.
                            I wanted eternity
with her, but I was not her owner, and soon—
with a jolt—like a joyful spirit she bolted
over, joining the plainer flock that waited
invisibly on the other side—like a bride—
and with her into the ether danced my pride
in having even briefly known her.

To a Wild Rose

"with simple tenderness," for Beth

It's true, what all our
heroes say. There *is* a way
in this world for beauty,
for good. It may
be a crooked path
in a tanglewood, but
stay the course and,
when the way grows rocky,
walk your horse,

and who knows, you may yet
come upon the wild rose,
as I have done, and,
paying close attention,
keep from crushing her into
the grime, and then,
with any luck, in time
remember how you found her
and how to find her again
when the way gets wilder.

One Can Miss Mountains

and pine. One

can dismiss
a whisper's

revelations
and go on as

before as if
everything were

perfectly fine.
One does. One

loses wonder
among stores

of things.
One can even miss

the basso boom
of the ocean's

rumpus room
and its rhythm.

A man can leave
this earth

and take nothing
—not even

longing—along
with him.

Enough

Enough is as good as a feast.
A bird is as good as a beast.
A morning's as good as a day.
Love me in your own way.

Acknowledgments

The author gratefully acknowledges the periodicals in which these poems first appeared:

Commonweal:	"Worst Work"
GSU Review:	"More So"
Missouri Review:	"To Wind a Mechanical Toy"
	"Yellowrocket"
New England Review:	"A Man Stares into the Same Painting Day after Day"
The New Yorker:	"One Can Miss Mountains"
Poetry:	"Ere We Are Aware"
	"How Smokes the Smolder"
	"Nocturne" under a different title
	"The Day Is Gray and the Lake"
	"The Hush of the Very Good"
	"White Ash Goes Up at a Touch"
Prairie Schooner:	"As in a Sudden Downpour, When"
Subtropics:	"Turbulence: Three Exercises"
The Sun:	"Another Hand"
Sycamore Review:	"Things, Like Dogs"
TriQuarterly:	"Constellations"
	"*Don't Come Home*"
	"The Deeper the Dictionary"
Virginia Quarterly Review:	"Advance"
	"In the Morning We Found"
	"Ruin"
	"The Plat Book"
Willow Springs:	"My Son Climbs In"
	"My House Is Small and Almost"

The following poems appeared in *On Marriage* (Red Dragonfly Press), a limited-edition letterpress chapbook co-written with poet Katrina Vandenberg: "*Don't Come Home*," "What Yesterday Appeared a Scar," "The Wallpaper," "Tangled Hangers and All," "Icicles."

Notes

Yellowrocket is the familiar name for *Barbarea vulgaris,* an invasive weed common to Wisconsin and the upper Midwest.

A plat book is a sectional map of land survey and ownership information county by county.

The plat book page that opens the first section of this book shows the locations of the original Wisconsin homesteads of my great great grandfather August and my great great great grandfather Carl. The three lots, labeled *Wiersig,* can be found near the middle of the page.

The storm in question is the windstorm of July 15, 1980—still the single worst natural disaster in Wisconsin state history.

"Chimney" is inspired by Edip Cansever's beautiful poem, "Table."

"A Deer" was commissioned by Constance Holmes to mark the eightieth birthday of poet Rosamond Rosenmeier and has been altered from the original. The line "It seems to me to be again as if" is taken from Rosenmeier's poem "Griefwork for My Mother," from *Lines Out* (Alice James, 1989).

"To a Wild Rose" takes its title from the piano composition of the same name by Edward MacDowell (1861–1908) in *Woodland Sketches,* op. 51.

Thanks

Foremost among my champions: Jack Miles, Polly Carl, Sherman Alexie, Anne Ylvisaker, Tom Keller III.

Editors who backed me with their good reputations: Carol Houck Smith, Christian Wiman and staff, Alice Quinn, Susan Firestone Hahn, C. Dale Young, Brett Ortler, Hilda Raz, Michael Callaghan, Sidney Wade.

Family that saw my work as important.

Writers who were generous toward me: Alicia Ostriker, Mark Doty, Jim Moore, Dick Allen, David Clewell, Terri Ford, Tony Hoagland, Philip Dacey, Thomas Lux, Carol Connolly, Dorianne Laux, Charles Martin, Jonis Agee, Jim Lenfestey, Katrina Vandenberg, Christine Rhein, Anna Ziegler, Liz Weir.

And others whose enthusiasms went a long way: Joan Lazarus; Rachel, Wayne, and Yvonne Greene; Eric Fawcett and Sarah Hauss; Katie Bratsch; Andrew Carroll; Sandy Clark; Emily Cook and Daniel Slager; Constance Holmes; Anne Klefstad; June Berkowitz at Nina's Café and Susan Zumberge at Common Good Books; Regula Russelle; Jeff Shotts; Dara Syrkin; Beth Dow; Nancy Stauffer Cahoon.

But most of all, I am grateful for the loving patience of my wife, Amy Grove.